Your Daily Dose of PositiviDee

Dee DiFatta

Green Heart Living Press

Your Daily Dose of PositiviDee

ISBN (paperback): 978-1-954493-01-8
ISBN (ebook): 978-1-954493-03-2

Cover photo by Dee DiFatta
Back Cover Portrait by Sandra Costello
Edited by Casey Banville

Dedication

To my soulmate Mike, I love you for supporting me and accepting me, flaws and all. You are a bright light in my world and I thank you for always loving and believing in me.

Introduction

In the past, I was so scared to be authentically me. I felt insecure, inadequate, and unworthy. I believed that I had to "Fit In" and please others in order to be loved and accepted. By the time I got to High School, I had become an overachieving stressed-out perfectionist, and I wore this as a badge of honor. When I did not feel overwhelmed, I felt like I wasn't doing enough. By going and doing, I felt worthy and depleted at the same time, I got lost in who I thought I "should be." And by being negative, fearful, and sarcastic, I created a painful reality.

It was not until I was diagnosed with Multiple Sclerosis a few months after I graduated college that I realized something had to change. I was awakened with a new awareness that I had been taking life for granted. Although we do not get to decide what we are challenged with in life, we have absolute control over how we deal with it. And I chose to be positive.

When I made this internal shift from fixating on what was going wrong to being grateful for every little thing in my life, my world changed. I began to see life from a new perspective. I realized that I was not destined to doom and gloom. I may not be able to change my past, but every day is a new day to script a new chapter in my story. I have redefined MS as Modified Swagger and Motivational Spitfire and I have redefined myself as "A Work in Progress."

I am blessed with the awareness that what you think, you create, and what you speak, you affirm. I have found my way out of the darkness and into a place of unlimited possibilities. And now that I have opened this gateway for myself, I am illuminating a path for others to access their boundless potential.

PositiviDee is not about rainbows and unicorns. PositiviDee is an attitude, an awareness, and a perspective. It illuminates you from the inside out and encourages, supports, and guides you to be authentically you. It is positively liberating because it gives you guidance to set yourself free from limiting self-doubts and insecurities. PositiviDee is an invitation to own your uniqueness and your potential for greatness.

January 1

Perspective and PositiviDee can inspire peace and harmony.

January 2

In order to receive, you must be open to receiving.

January 3

Life doesn't come with a script or an instruction manual. You are the author of your own story.

January 4

"Normal" is boring. Keep life interesting by embracing your abnormalities and celebrating your uniqueness.

January 5

When you are enduring life, you block your blessings.
But when you embrace life, a gateway opens to endless possibilities. So, don't just endure life; embrace it.

January 6

In order to "Go with the flow," you must be able to let your perfectly detailed agenda go. Sometimes the things that happen spontaneously are even better than what you had originally planned.

January 7

Try laughing at your unforeseen circumstances from time to time.
Humor can be incredibly healing.

January 8

This too shall pass. Maybe not today and maybe not tomorrow, but this too shall pass eventually.

January 9

Rest and reflection produce revelations.

January 10

The more you affirm, "I am proud to be authentically me," the more it becomes your reality.

January 11

Every journey begins with a single step. And every dream requires a leap of faith.

January 12

Surround yourself with a positive community. They will inspire you to learn more, love deeper, and accept yourself for who you are.

January 13

We all have our own unique crosses to bear whether they belong to us personally or we are carrying them for other people.
But if we take life one minute at a time, it makes it easier to keep things in perspective and persevere.

January 14

By trying to
"Fit In,"
we lose a part of
ourselves.
Don't allow
social anxiety and peer
pressure to coerce you
into being ordinary.
You were born to be
EXTRAordinary!

January 15

Challenge
yourself to
experience
new things
outside of the
safety bubble you
have created for
yourself.

January 16

Be curious as to what lies on the other side of your comfort zone.

January 17

You are not limited by your limitations.

January 18

So many of our fears
are exacerbated by
our own thoughts
and judgements.
Just remember that
fears are not facts.
They are just beliefs.
And YOU have the
power to fuel them
or diffuse them.

January 19

Don't be afraid to share your story.
A bad chapter in your life can be an inspiration to someone else.

January 20

Your spirit can be bruised, but it can never be broken.

January 21

Have fun with the journey. Life is not all about the destination.

January 22

By re-defining yourself as "A Work in Progress," you can let perfection go and allow your potential to flow.

January 23

Everything you have
experienced in your
lifetime,
(the good, the bad,
and the ugly),
has played a part in
who you are today.
And when you look back
and observe the
BIG picture,
it's magnificent and
so are you.

January 24

The only way
anyone or
anything can
bring you down
is if you let
them,
and that is not
an option.

January 25

It's time to release your attachment to how other people perceive you and stand confident and courageous in the truth of your being. You were not born to be a follower. You were born to be a leader and show others the way.

January 26

Nurture your spirit by focusing on simple things that bring you joy.
For instance, pet a dog or a cat. Watch a funny video. Spend time outside observing the beauty of nature.

January 27

As you go through life,
do not lose sight of your dreams.
Sometimes we get so
overwhelmed with
our day jobs, our families,
our chores, and our obligations
that we put our dreams on hold
indefinitely.
You don't have to clear your
head and your calendar
in order to nurture your dreams.
Just be consciously aware of
setting boundaries and making
your dreams a priority.

January 28

Give yourself permission to take a break and take care of yourself.
No one else knows what you need more than you do.

January 29

Asking for help is a sign of strength, not weakness.

January 30

Don't compare yourself to anyone else.
No two humans are exactly alike.
We are all at different stages in our self-discovery journeys.

January 31

Challenge yourself to learn or do something new every day.
By staying curious, you build the muscles in your mind and you move forward with more confidence and momentum.

February 1

Tell fear that its reign of power is over. Your indomitable spirit is taking over.

February 2

In order to truly grow,
you must be willing to let go of the status quo and allow your creativity to flow.

February 3

Struggles are not meant to stop you. They are meant to make you stronger.

February 4

Always seek to understand. Stop assuming you know it all and allow yourself to entertain different perspectives.

February 5

You don't have control over people's actions, but you have absolute control over your reactions.

February 6

Lean into change. Evolution is empowering.

February 7

Your purpose is to trust and accept who you are in this moment and set an intention for who you want to become moving forward.

February 8

By believing in yourself and having faith, anything is possible.

February 9

Connecting with others and sharing your stories is food for the soul.

February 10

Just because you live in a world of immediate gratification, does not mean that you can expect change and transformation to happen right away. The seeds must be planted and given time to grow.

February 11

Adopt a positive attitude by focusing on gratitude.

February 12

Try adjusting your mindset to create a shift in momentum.

February 13

In order to turn up the volume and the vision of your deepest desires, you may have to turn up your vibrations. Surround yourself with things that bring you joy.

February 14

Always seek to set the bar higher than your comfort level. By aiming higher, you will be more empowered and feel increasingly energized.

February 15

You were born into a world of infinite color and possibilities. Don't get stuck living in the grayscale.

February 16

A butterfly cannot transition back to a caterpillar,
and you were not meant to convert back to the old version of yourself either.
Keep evolving and moving forward.

February 17

Don't allow yourself to get consumed by the material world.
You are just the consumer.

February 18

You can fixate on life being tragic, or you can focus on life being full of magic.
But be forewarned, your energy flows where your attention goes.

February 19

If you want to change how you see the world, you must allow yourself to go within and be the change.

February 20

When you are optimistic and determined, growth will lead to greatness.

February 21

Stop dreaming about
what you want to do in
life and just do it.
Set an intention
and commit to it.
You don't have to know
how to make your
dreams come true.
Just take consistent
action every day,
and your plans will
come together before
your eyes.

February 22

Believe in what you cannot see, and it will be. There is magic everywhere.

February 23

It's easier to travel
with less baggage and
negativity weighing
you down.
So, before you leave
the house,
pack your bags with
confidence and
courage,
and leave the
self-doubts and worry
behind.

February 24

True love is an inside job. You were born loved, loving, and lovable.

February 25

Bring the S.M.I.L.E. factor into your life.
Self-Awareness
Motivation
Inspiration
Love
Empowerment

February 26

Although you may
seek love, acceptance,
and validation
from others,
they all exist
within you.
In order to
access them,
you must spend some
quiet time with
yourself.

March 1

Whether you are taking one step forward or ten steps backward, you are still moving.
Be grateful in the process of your journey.

February 29

Have FUN getting things done.
You do not have to treat everything in life as a chore or an obligation.

February 28

The past has passed. Focus your attention on what you can do in the present to elevate you to the next level in the future.

Change does not bring pain. It's the resistance to change that causes discomfort and frustration.

March 2

You are going to receive life advice from countless people.
Take what you need and leave the rest behind.
You are not obliged to follow the leader.
You are the leader.

March 3

Your insecurities can cripple your creativity.
Be aware of how you are feeling and if you feel stuck, stop, pause, and re-adjust.

March 4

Love gives us the power to overcome every challenge we face.

March 5

In order to stay confident,
stop comparing
yourself to other
people and only
compare yourself to
who you were
yesterday.
If you are not happy
with the progress you
are making,
stop, pause, and
re-evaluate your path.

March 6

Befriend your
fears and allow
yourself
to steer.
Put fear in the
backseat and
take your power
back.

March 7

Allow yourself to take a deep cleansing breath. Breathe in through your nose and out through your mouth. Do this again and pay attention to how you feel. Breathing inspires healing. It has the power to refresh and renew your mind, body, and spirit.

March 8

When you feel depleted and out of energy, stop, pause, and breathe. You need to recharge your batteries.

March 9

You may have big plans for yourself but sometimes the Universe has even bigger plans for you. Don't allow yourself to feel rejected or dejected if your plans don't work out. Just keep thinking that something better is just around the corner.

March 10

Keep in mind that spirituality is not the same thing as religion. You do not need to belong to a church in order to believe in a Higher Power. No matter your frustration or dis-connect with religion, spirituality is all loving and accepting.

March 11

Just because someone
told you to be quiet in
the past,
does not mean you
have to silence
yourself going
forward.
Your voice matters
and if you feel
inspired to share
something,
speak up and speak
out.

March 12

When things seem bleak,
look back on how far
you have already
come on your
journey.
You are amazingly
resilient.
Stay focused on your
purpose and
persevere.

March 13

Give others the
opportunity to choose
their path in life.
Everyone needs to be free
to make their own
mistakes
in order to learn new
lessons and get stronger.
Stay focused on your story
and lead by example.
You are a better guide
when you walk the walk
you speak than by just
talking the talk you
believe.

March 14

Always be open to constructive criticism. No matter how brilliant you are, you do not know everything.

March 15

In order to access your power within, you must first take responsibility for your life and the choices you make.

March 16

Life is not always rainbows
and unicorns,
but it's not always the
constant struggle and crisis
we perceive it to be either.
Darkness and light exist
within you and around you at
the same time.
And YOU HAVE THE
POWER TO CHOOSE!
Are you going to choose to
stay in the darkness and
suffer?
Or are you going to choose to
dig deep,
turn up the light within you,
and shine bright?

March 17

Allow yourself to dream big. And then, commit and act on your big dreams.

March 18

Stop sitting on your assets and move forward with confidence.

March 19

Don't beat yourself up for resisting transformation. It is challenging to let go of who you have always been and embrace who you are becoming. Give yourself time to adjust and accept the process.

March 20

Give your mind a break.
Even computers need time to reboot.
Sometimes the answers you seek appear when you are resting.

March 21

As you become awakened to new awareness and different perspectives, a gateway opens to your unlimited potential.

March 22

You have the power to create your reality with your thoughts, words, and actions. Always strive to create peace and joy by living in harmony and enthusiasm.

March 23

Be ready to release the familiar in order to embrace the fabulous.

March 24

Your perceptions are based on beliefs. They exist only in your mind. Don't allow these illusions to create confusion.

March 25

In order to find peace in the world, you must first be at peace with yourself.

March 26

As changes occur in your life, trust that the Universe is guiding you towards new beginnings that will be better aligned with your purpose and passion.

March 27

Just because you have always been a certain way, does not mean you have to stay that way forever.
You get to choose who and how you want to be.

March 28

When you feel uncomfortable in your own skin and you feel out of balance, chances are that you have evolved and grown out of something in your life. Allow yourself time to ponder this situation and then persevere.

March 29

The path to self-discovery and enlightenment is guided by the Universe.
So, don't be surprised when you have to take a U turn.
The path you seek lies within.

March 30

You have most likely modeled your life after the people you learned from growing up.
But always be open to new ideas, perspectives and possibilities so you can continue to grow.

March 31

Your body gets stiff when you don't stretch it and your mindset gets rigid when you think the same thoughts every day.
It's time to start doing some mental exercises and loosen things up by entertaining new perspectives.

April 1

By keeping
things in
perspective,
you can
maintain a
positive spirit
amidst
challenging
situations.

April 2

Stop blaming others for your circumstances. Once you take responsibility for your actions, you are no longer the victim. You are the victor.

April 3

Your possessions may bring you fleeting happiness but joy cannot be bought. It is your birthright.

April 4

Your self-doubts,
fears and worries
are not facts.
They are limiting
beliefs that
have been learned
over time.
You have the power
to unlearn them and
move forward with
confidence and
courage.

April 5

Don't allow your beautiful spirit to be held captive.
It's time to master your thoughts instead of allowing them to master you.

April 6

You are worthy of self-care, self-love, self-respect, and self-acceptance. So, feel free to embrace being self-ish.

April 7

When you feel like you are having an identity crisis, you are most likely in a state of transition.
Be patient with yourself and get ready for the new and improved you.

April 8

A lot of times we hear something,
we internalize it,
and we allow it to turn into something much bigger than it was ever intended to be.
Don't allow a negative comment or thought to become a big monster in your mind.

April 9

Your indomitable spirit makes you a superhero. When things get tough, it can step in and build you up.

April 10

Living is so much more than going, doing, and being. It is also the constant process of accepting, forgiving, releasing, and becoming.

April 11

You are being called to thrive, not just survive.

Your Daily Dose of PositiviDee

April 12

Every day is an opportunity to live your best life. Choose to live in the magic instead of the mayhem.

April 13

Don't be ashamed of your past.
You are a blessing and your backstory is an inspiration to others.

April 14

It's time to set yourself FREE with forgiveness and authenticity.

April 15

Stop creating obstacles for yourself to overcome. Let your excuses go and choose to live in the flow.

April 16

As a child growing up, you may have been required to ask permission to pee. But as an adult, you do not have to ask permission from anyone to just BE. You have 100% authority.

April 17

Serving others is acceptable. Sacrificing yourself is not.

April 18

Give your inner child permission to come out and play with you. Re-ignite your curiosity, creativity, and imagination.

April 19

Love and compassion are strong emotions. Do not fear their power. Have faith, open your heart, and lean into infinite possibilities.

April 20

You have the capacity to heal but you must be open to receive before your healing journey can begin.

April 21

By thinking about the past and fretting about the future, you miss out on the opportunities in the present.

April 22

Living in this
new world of
"Political Correctness" has
limited our capacity of
curiosity and
understanding.
Instead of asking questions,
we assume.
And instead of promoting
inclusion,
we are unconsciously
encouraging exclusion.
Give yourself permission to
explore new possibilities.

April 23

You have the power to choose how you see yourself and how you see the world.
Do not limit yourself to the standards set by society.

April 24

Change can be scary but staying the same can be even more terrifying.

April 25

Do not let your limiting beliefs hold your unlimited potential hostage.

April 26

Self-confidence should be built from the inside out and not from the outside in.

April 27

You can't turn back time and make changes to the past. But you can start making changes going forward.

April 28

Fear of the unknown can be daunting but it's just a belief. Dig deep and give yourself permission to believe that better things are on the other side of this fear you are feeling.

April 29

Aspire to Inspire.

April 30

If H.E.L.P. was redefined as Healing Energy Loving Perspective, I bet you would ask for it more often.

May 1

You are in a constant state of metamorphosis. Be kind and gentle with yourself as you go through your life journey.

May 2

Instead of fixating on what you don't have, be grateful for everything you do have and start visualizing what you want to manifest.

May 3

Once you engage your spirituality, the signs and synchronicities sent by the Universe start to come into focus.
You can see things from a different perspective.
And life becomes magical.

May 4

When you are feeling challenged with an uncomfortable, painful, or difficult situation, have faith that the Universe is preparing you for something greater in your life.

May 5

True healing requires more than a Band-Aid™. It is not an outside job.
It starts on the inside with your thoughts and feelings.

May 6

Vulnerability is not a weakness. It takes immense inner strength to share your authenticity with others.

May 7

Your thoughts can be more debilitating and demoralizing than anything anyone else could ever say to you.
If you wouldn't share your thoughts with a friend in need,
don't share them with yourself either.

May 8

You are more important than you can ever imagine. Don't ever underestimate yourself or your reason for living.

May 9

Don't ever beat yourself up for the progress you are making. Every baby step is a positive step forward.

May 10

If you are too tired to take a step, take a nap. Honor your body and rest and relax so you can be rejuvenated for your journey.

May 11

Give yourself permission to scrap the "To Do List" and take care of you instead.

May 12

Make your health a priority so you can keep up with yourself and your evolution.

May 13

In order to find
the light,
take down the
walls and the
barricades you put
up to keep
yourself safe.
Allow the beautiful
light within you to
shine bright.

May 14

Don't dim your light or diminish your sparkle.

May 15

Sometimes you need to surrender control and ask for guidance. Then, be silent and listen for the answers.

May 16

When you are on "The Edge of Glory," don't allow fear and your ego to step in and talk you off the ledge.
Just Jump!

May 17

Do not allow your past to
dictate your future.
You may still be carrying
old thoughts and feelings
around with you,
but they cannot hurt you
unless you give them
power.
You have grown into a
magnificent being.
Stand in your truth,
own and affirm your
gifts and talents,
and keep moving
forward.

May 18

You have the power to heal and hurt with your words, thoughts, and actions.
Stay consciously aware and choose wisely.

May 19

Shame and blame
are lame.
They are not serving
you or helping
anyone else.
Thank them for
coming and tell them
to move on out.
Make some new
room for love and
acceptance in your
life.

May 20

Learn to laugh at your blooper moments and share them with others. Make them part of your story.

May 21

Even though it seems as if our world is being turned upside down and we are just along for
the ride,
we are growing stronger and stronger every day as we navigate our struggles.

May 22

There is always hope but first you must embrace your own power to stay afloat.

May 23

Make a commitment to yourself and this nation to seek out the positivity in everyone and everything.
Take a stand and rise up to the challenge of being a leader in this world.

May 24

Eliminate clutter to amplify clarity.
By releasing what is no longer serving you, energy and confidence is restored.

May 25

You have the power to make life-changing shifts happen!

May 26

Spirituality is the connection between you and your Higher Self. If you allow it into your life, it will guide you on your divine path.

May 27

A little gratitude can shift your entire attitude.

May 28

It's always better to under-promise and over-deliver than it is to over-promise and under-deliver.

May 29

Sometimes you have to say "No" to good things so you can say "Yes" to better things.

May 30

The only person who has the authority to define you and your abilities is YOU.

May 31

Don't allow yourself to be consumed by who you think you should be or what you think you should be doing. Focus on who you are in this moment and what you want to manifest going forward.

June 1

When you know what you want, share it with others. Ask for assistance and expect good things to happen.

June 2

The power of perspective is all about shifting your mindset. You have the ability to choose and shift from self-sabotage to self-care, surviving to thriving and so much more.

June 3

It's time to believe in you and what you can do. By changing the conversation in your head from "I can't" to "I can," you unlock a portal of unlimited potential.

June 4

Your spirituality is based on your individuality. It is unique to you.

June 5

Reasoning creates resistance. Allow yourself the freedom to have fun and think outside of the box.

June 6

Sometimes the tighter you hold onto things, the faster they crumble. Trust in the bigger plan that the Universe has for you.

June 7

Your reality is
limited by your
five senses,
but your truth is
only limited by your
imagination.
Give yourself
permission to think
big and unleash the
amazing person you
were born to be.

June 8

Truth be told... you may be more terrified of unimaginable success than you are of failure. But no need to worry. You've got this!

June 9

You are exactly where you are meant to be at this exact moment in time.

June 10

Try accepting
yourself for once.
There are enough
people in the world
who are going to
judge you based on
perceptions they
inherited from
the past.
You don't have to be
one of them.

June 11

Being in harmony with yourself and the world around you is a fundamental step in building a strong foundation for transformation.

June 12

Just because you
have a different
perspective than
everyone else
around you,
does not make you
right or wrong.
You are unique.
You have a right to
your own opinions.

June 13

Allow yourself to be authentic and vulnerable. By revealing who you really are, it eliminates the need to judge and hold a grudge.

June 14

There is no need to beat yourself up for doing something "out of character." There is beauty in improvisation.

June 15

One little shift can create a huge impact.

June 16

Work on cultivating the love within yourself before you try to teach others how to find it.

June 17

More magic is found in the mistakes than in the masterpieces.

June 18

When you give, you also receive. So, share some love and light and watch your world grow bright.

June 19

Pushing through is not always the best thing to do. Give yourself permission to take a step back and assess the situation before you decide to keep moving forward.

June 20

Be grateful for every roadblock you encounter. They exist to re-direct you on your journey and re-fuel your passion to keep going.

June 21

You are connected to a Higher Power, but you need to wake up from your conditioned coma to feel the energy and receive your true calling.

June 22

Believe in your unlimited truth and tell the Universe to "Bring it on." Commit to taking action to make it happen.

June 23

Before you can learn new things, you sometimes need to unlearn old things.

June 24

Embrace F.A.I.T.H. Fundamental Awareness Inspires True Healing

June 25

Cut the crap and take your power back. You have free will to make your own decisions so make them.

June 26

Would you consciously put yourself in shackles and chains and send yourself to prison for all eternity for saying the wrong thing or making a minor mistake? No?! Then, consciously forgive yourself for harboring guilt and resentment and set yourself free to just be.

June 27

Being worried is
a habit.
It is not a
state of being.
Choose to release
your worries to the
Universe and
replace them with
love for yourself
and your situation.

June 28

Every time you believe and repeat something negative about yourself,
you chip away at your self-love and wellbeing.
Choose to love yourself –
flaws and all.

June 29

Be open to more good than you can imagine.

June 30

Just because other people don't share your enthusiasm for your little wins in life, does not mean you shouldn't celebrate.

July 1

Live in the moment and listen to your body
If you want to dance, DANCE.
If you want to sing, SING.
If you want to sleep, SLEEP.
Be true to you.

July 2

Don't allow yourself to get so consumed making a living that you forget to live life to the fullest.

July 3

Dealing with adversity makes you aware of your power to persevere.

July 4

Judgements and expectations lead to disappointment and frustrations. Choose love and gratitude and amplify your mood and attitude.

July 5

There is no need to wait around for a hero when you have the capability to save yourself.

July 6

Your mindset is the only thing holding you back from turning up the volume and the vision of your deepest desires. Stop holding yourself hostage and affirm your brilliance.

July 7

Your brain believes whatever you tell it. So, make sure you are telling stories of encouragement, support, inspiration, and positivity.

July 8

You may be a victim of circumstance, but you do not have to live in victim mode. You were born to be an inspiration.

July 9

When you get stuck, readjust.

July 10

You've got this! You have always had this! Sometimes you just need a friendly reminder.

July 11

Stop making life more complicated than it already is. Focus on what is going right in your life and be grateful for this opportunity to live life to the fullest.

July 12

Awareness is the first step to self-discovery.

July 13

Life is too short to surround yourself with people who suck the life out of you. Spend time with people who build you up and make you feel special.

July 14

When you find acceptance from within, you will no longer feel compelled to seek it elsewhere.

July 15

You are not a robot and you were not programmed to do everything all by yourself. Help yourself and ask for help.

July 16

No one knows you better than you know yourself. Don't let anyone else tell you who you are or what you want. You are the boss of you.

July 17

When you give yourself permission to love yourself, you gain more control over your life.

July 18

You have the power to blaze your own path and become who you want to be.

July 19

Surround yourself with people who will support, encourage, and motivate you to keep moving forward.

July 20

You are free to pivot and pursue other possibilities.

July 21

Trust and believe in the flow so you can grow and go. By waiting for approval and validation, you get stuck in the status quo.

July 22

Always listen to your intuition before you make a big decision.

July 23

There is no such thing as a Fairy Godmother and "Bibbidi Bobbidi Boo." But you have absolute authority to Bibbidi Bobbidi Do You.

July 24

You are surrounded by friends and family who want what's best for you. But don't allow yourself to get sucked into their hopes and dreams. Stay true to you and what you want to do.

July 25

Every day has the potential to be a great day.

July 26

Think bigger than
you are today.
What you think,
you create.
So, stop playing
small and stretch
your imagination.

July 27

Being true to you will attract a tribe that is right for you.

July 28

No need to deny your individuality.

July 29

There are always at least two sides to every story. Stay open to receive all the information so you can make the best decision.

Your Daily Dose of PositiviDee

July 30

In order to see more, take your blinders off and look around. Utilize your peripheral vision.

July 31

Although you may feel broken, you have the power to put yourself back together even better than before.

August 1

You will face situations that test your resolve, but you are amazingly resilient. You are stronger than you think.

August 2

You may fail but you are not a failure.

August 3

Acknowledge and appreciate your past so you can trust and accept your present and create your future with confidence and clarity.

August 4

Bliss appears when you stop dissing yourself with your thoughts, words, and actions.

It's time to rise out of the darkness and invite in the light.

August 6

Sometimes you must figure out what doesn't work for you before you discover what does.

August 7

Self-acceptance is possible, but it is a process.
Be patient and kind with yourself while you are going through your transformation.

August 8

You don't have to wipe the slate clean to start over. Becoming a better version of yourself starts with awareness and perspective. And sometimes one tiny shift can make a huge impact and catapult you in the right direction.

August 9

You have not
lost your
identity.
You have only
lost your way.
Your true
essence
lies within.

August 10

Do not allow negative energy to derail you.

August 11

Your need for love, approval, and validation have made you vulnerable to rejection. But just know that the connection you have to your spirituality and the Universe is your protection.

August 12

Start to appreciate the little things in life so you can truly appreciate everything in life.

Your Daily Dose of PositiviDee

August 13

Progress takes patience and persistence.

August 14

It is never too late to find your purpose and passion. You are special and have a lot to offer this world.

August 15

Life is an adventure. Allow yourself to live it!

August 16

Most party invitations have a start time and an end time.
If you are going to have a pity party for yourself, make sure you schedule an end time.

August 17

You were born with a bright light inside of you. But it's on a dimmer switch. Turn it all the way up and shine bright.

August 18

Simple acts of kindness go a long way, especially when they get paid forward.

August 19

Possibility is defined by your perspective.

August 20

You must consciously take your blinders off and step off the hamster wheel in order to see the blessings before you.

August 21

Little adjustments to your thinking will inspire big shifts in your behavior.

August 22

You were born a superhero. You have just misplaced your superpower.

August 23

You have the power within you to stop the madness around you by minding your own business.

August 24

By unconsciously reacting to a situation instead of consciously responding, you relinquish control.

August 25

Stepping into the energy of curiosity inspires abundance.

August 26

When everyone and everything is driving you nuts, it's time to take a break. 99% of the time it's not them; it's you. (You are the common denominator.)

August 27

Turn up your vibration and get ready to experience life from a higher elevation.

August 28

It's OK to set boundaries and create time and space for yourself.

August 29

Time-outs aren't just good for kids. They are fantastic for grown-ups too.

August 30

Your dreams
are not going
to come true
without you.
Take action
and make
decisions
about your
visions.

August 31

You have the power to weave your own destiny.

September 1

Be careful what you tell yourself because your brain believes it and creates more of it for you.

September 2

Don't allow the word "No" to deter you from living your dreams. Let it inspire you toward your "Yes."

September 3

Transformation is not always pretty. Sometimes you feel wonky and wobbly and that's OK. Just hold on for another day.

September 4

At your core, you are so much more.

September 5

When you want, you come from scarcity and lack. When you affirm, you already own it.

September 6

Thoughts and words trigger us into action.
So, be sure to focus on positivity so you can inspire more confidence and clarity.

September 7

Instead of putting off your burdens and allowing them to have power over you, take control and get things accomplished so there is no contest. You win!

September 8

Before you take action to throw it all away, seek to understand and find another way.

September 9

Always have faith in a higher power. Whether you believe in God, Universe, Spirit, Source, etc., He/She/It always has your back.

September 10

If you want to master life, you must first master your mind.

September 11

Give yourself permission to experience limitless health, wealth, and abundance. Own it, affirm it, and expect more of it.

September 12

Up until now,
you may have been
M.I.A. (Missing It
Altogether.)
But it's never too
late to redirect your
attention and A.I.M.
(Adjust Intentions
Mindfully)
for something
bigger and better.

September 13

You always have the opportunity to reclaim your power and reclaim your life. The question is, "Are you ready?"

Your Daily Dose of PositiviDee

September 14

Before you start
your day,
check your
perceptions,
judgements,
limiting beliefs,
self-doubts, and
fears at the door
and choose to move
forward with a
positive perspective.

September 15

Don't get so fixated looking for answers that you lose sight of the signs that are being sent to guide you.

September 16

It can be challenging to trust and believe in the unseen and the unknown. But once you do, your entire world changes from limited to limitless.

September 17

Habits are hard to break.
But they can be broken by changing your thought process. Believe and it shall become true.

September 18

On your list of priorities, where are you on it?
If you are not at the top of the list, it's time to make an adjustment.

September 19

In order to get aligned with the Divine, it's always good to get organized.

September 20

Heal your ideals by embracing life for what it is and not what you think it should be.

September 21

You don't need to take time off to take a self-care break. When you take time for you, even if it's just thirty seconds, make sure you stay focused on the moment and be true to you and what you need.

September 22

Instead of saying,
"I'm overwhelmed" and
feeling stressed out and
anxious about
your situation,
try saying something
more positive.
Try affirming,
"I am blessed with
countless opportunities
and I am grateful
to be busy."
And see how this shifts
your perspective.

September 23

You do not need permission to love yourself completely. You are worthy and deserving of more love than you can imagine.

September 24

Forgiveness inspires personal freedom and forward momentum.

September 25

Instead of peer pressure, let's show some peer support.

September 26

Choose collaboration over competition.

September 27

When you feel stuck and out of control in your own life, don't try to make yourself feel better by fixing someone else's problems. Stop, pause, and go within.

September 28

Stop fixating on counting your calories and count your blessings instead.

September 29

It can be so much easier to say "Yes" to someone else. But now is the time to flip the script. You are worthy and deserving of saying "Yes" to you first.

September 30

Your learned perceptions and limiting beliefs have the power to create your reality.
Be aware this is not your divine truth.

October 1

Instead of getting frustrated with your momentum, focus on all the progress you have already made.

October 2

Sometimes when you take a break and have some fun, you open up and the ideas come.

October 3

By taking
responsibility for
your life and
claiming
everything to be a
lesson
or a blessing,
you deny that
anyone or
anything else has
power over you.

October 4

When you forgive yourself and others, you open a gateway to peace, love, and healing.

October 5

Believe in Divine timing. Don't try to force things. Stay calm and watch things evolve.

October 6

Don't allow yourself to unconsciously go with the flow. Always try to be consciously aware and choose where to go.

October 7

You are free to re-define your circumstances, get re-aligned with your purpose, and re-design your path at any time.

October 8

When you are full of love and gratitude, there is no room for negativity and self-doubt.

October 9

Redefine BS so you can reclaim your power and reclaim your life.
No more
<u>B</u>ull **<u>S</u>**h#$.
It's time to make shifts in your mind and let your
<u>B</u>eautiful **<u>S</u>**pirit shine.

October 10

Your energy is attached to everything. If something is draining you, let it go.

October 11

Stop waiting and anticipating. Start acting and make good things happen.

October 12

Everybody has an opinion,
but you don't have to let them sway your decisions.
Trust your instinct and follow your intuition.

October 13

In order to modify your behavior, you must first adjust your thought process.

October 14

Don't get stuck in rationalizing everything. Too much analysis leads to momentum paralysis.

October 15

Your self-discovery journey is all about you. Don't compare yourself to anyone else.

October 16

As you set intentions and do what you love, you will be more aligned with your purpose and passion.
And this is when the magic happens.

October 17

You don't have to have all the answers. Focus on the gifts God gave you and ask for help with everything else.

October 18

Clarity and confidence are found in community, connection, and collaborations. You are not alone on your journey through life.

October 19

You are so much more than your reflection in the mirror. You are a warrior and a hero. Stand proud and own your superpowers.

October 20

Social media is a platform for connections and outreach. It is not a place to seek acceptance and validation.

October 21

When you learn to embrace your beautiful spirit, others will too.

October 22

By making more of an effort, there is less room for excuses.

October 23

In order to understand and appreciate the world around you, explore what is happening within you.

October 24

The good you do in this world never dies. It lives on in other people.

October 25

Don't expect too much from your heroes and not enough from yourself.

October 26

Your future is a mystery. Have patience and give yourself permission to create and experience your destiny.

October 27

Design your dream and set your intentions. By plotting your course, it's easier to stay focused and aligned.

October 28

When you focus on your problems, this becomes your reality. Instead of allowing your problems to become your pitfalls, focus on what you have learned from them and look for the opportunities they create.

October 29

You are not spiraling out of control. You are just spinning in a circle of limiting beliefs. Take some time to pause, reflect, and observe and make a conscious choice to step outside of the situation.

October 30

The way you think and the things you think about have a profound impact on your health and wellbeing.

October 31

Nourish your body, mind, and spirit with love, appreciation, and acceptance.

November 1

Your old habits are not meant to serve you throughout your lifetime. Be bold and brave and try something new today.

November 2

Release your expectations and surrender to the process of transformation.

November 3

You are
surrounded by
abundance,
but it's on a
different
frequency.
Seek out some
inspiration to
raise your
vibrations.

November 4

Learn to love and respect yourself the way you love and respect others.

November 5

Do your best and lean into success.

November 6

Drop the facades and speak from your heart.

November 7

It's OK to feel frustrated but it's not OK to beat yourself up about it.

November 8

Give yourself time and space to feel what you are feeling so you can deal with it. Then let it go so you can be back in the flow.

November 9

Love, light, peace, and joy is your birthright.

Who are you to block your blessings and keep your wisdom and self-knowledge a secret?

November 11

Utilize your intention as your compass to the true you. It sets you free from your self-inflicted captivity.

November 12

Forgive yourself weak moments of disbelief and distrust that you are not enough.

November 13

Lean into your dream and ignite your passion for life.

November 14

Be curious about the future and build some excitement today for tomorrow.

November 15

Learn to adapt and make modifications to ever-changing situations.

November 16

Celebrate yourself in some way every day.

November 17

Breakdowns inspire blessings and breakthroughs.

November 18

You have the power to empower yourself.

November 19

Your breath is your connection to life, love, and light.
It can be as powerful as you can imagine.

You cannot go back and change your past, but you do have the ability to create your future.

November 21

By helping
yourself,
you are helping
others.
Your commitment
to self-care
ensures that you
will always have
something to
share.

November 22

Life is full of choices but it's up to you to choose.

November 23

It is not your
responsibility
to make sure
everyone else
feels safe
and secure.
Don't lose
yourself playing
God for others.

Your Daily Dose of PositiviDee

November 24

You are awake, alive, and aware. Now claim your greatness and get out there.

November 25

Awareness is the key to unlocking the infinite truth within you.

November 26

When you reconnect and re-ignite the light within you, the outside world gets brighter.

November 27

Set your mind free from captivity. Only you have the key to change your reality.

November 28

Words are just words. They have negative or positive connotations based on learned associations.

November 29

Every new day is a new beginning.

November 30

You always have the opportunity to step out of the old and into the new.

December 1

Get out of your head and into your happy zone.

December 2

Worthiness and wellbeing lie within.

December 3

It's never too late to retrain the brain and live life to the fullest.

December 4

Always be proud of your progress.

December 5

Show yourself some care and compassion.

December 6

You are a role model whether you like it or not so teach by example.

December 7

God loves you but He can only guide you with your consent.

December 8

A little gratitude can sky-rocket your attitude.

December 9

Obstacles can be transformed into opportunities with some faith and positivity.

December 10

Release the past with forgiveness. Embrace the present with gratitude. And design the future with intentions.

December 11

Be grateful in the process, trust the journey, and keep moving forward.

December 12

Every baby step is a gateway to big shifts.

December 13

Living is the constant process of becoming.

December 14

You learn as you grow and it's time to forgive yourself for what you did not know.

December 15

Worthiness is not calculated by your net worth.

December 16

When things appear to be falling apart, they are actually falling into place.

December 17

Failing inspires success. And "No" inspires "Yes."

December 18

Bliss lies on the other side of your imaginary fortress.

December 19

In order to heal the disconnect, you must take time to reflect.

December 20

Every ordeal offers the opportunity to heal.

December 21

You may have grown up in lack and scarcity but this is not your destiny.

December 22

Don't fight your insight.

December 23

Awareness inspires awakenings and abundance.

December 24

You were born with the drive to thrive.

December 25

Put your attention on your intention to guide your direction.

December 26

When you break through the resistance, you will experience redemption.

December 27

Be not afraid to affirm your inner strength.

December 28

Your greatness cannot be achieved in mediocrity.

December 29

Do not allow your negative thoughts to hold you back from living your dream.

December 30

What you think, you create and what you speak, you affirm.

December 31

Endings inspire new beginnings.

Your Daily Dose of PositiviDee

About Dee DiFatta

Dee DiFatta is a Perspective & PositiviDee Coach
and Founder of A Dose of PositiviDee. After 49
years of life, 27 years living with Multiple
Sclerosis, and 17 years working full-time in the
insurance industry, Dee has become a catalyst for
healing and positive change. Through private &
group coaching, educational programs, published
books, and speaking engagements, she helps
people redefine their circumstances so they can
break through their barriers and achieve
boundless potential. She teaches the
fundamental strategies necessary for people to
free themselves from their limiting beliefs of the
past and gain the confidence and courage to get
realigned with their purpose so they can redesign
their path forward.

To learn more about Dee and PositiviDee,
you can follow her at:

www.adoseofpositividee.com
facebook.com/deedifatta
facebook.com/adoseofpositividee
linkedin.com/in/dee-difatta/

About Green Heart Living

Green Heart Living's mission is to make the world a more loving and peaceful place, one person at a time. Green Heart Living Press publishes inspirational books and stories of transformation, making the world a more loving and peaceful place, one book at a time.

Whether you have an idea for an inspirational book and want support through the writing process - or your book is already written and you are looking for a publishing path - Green Heart Living can help you get your book out into the world.

You can meet Green Heart authors on the Green Heart Living YouTube channel and the Green Heart Living podcast.

www.greenheartliving.com

Green Heart Living Press Publications

Redefining Masculinity:
Visions for a New Way of Being

Grow Smarter: Collaboration Secrets to Transform
Your Income and Impact

Transformation 2020

Transformation 2020 Companion Journal

The Great Pause: Blessings & Wisdom from
COVID-19

The Great Pause Journal

Love Notes: Daily Wisdom for the Soul

Green Your Heart, Green Your World:
Avoid Burnout, Save the World and Love Your Life

www.greenheartliving.com

Made in United States
North Haven, CT
21 September 2022

24370985R00205